Published by Creative Education
123 South Broad Street, Mankato, Minnesota 56001
Creative Education is an imprint of The Creative Company

Designed by Stephanie Blumenthal
Production Design by The Design Lab
Editorial Assistance by Julie Bach

Photos by: AP/Wide World Photos, Archive Photos, Camera Press,
DMI Photos, Everett Collection, Globe Photos, Photofest, Shooting Star,
Retna Ltd., Rex USA Ltd.

Library of Congress Cataloging-in-Publication Data

DeBoer, Judy.
Whoopi Goldberg / by Judy DeBoer
p. cm. – (Ovations)
Summary: Describes the life of the stand-up comic and Hollywood
entertainer from her childhood to her current career.
ISBN 0-88682-696-9

1. Goldberg, Whoopi, 1950– –Juvenile literature. 2. Comedians–
United States–Biography–Juvenile literature. 3. Afro-American
comedians–United States–Biography–Juvenile literature. 4. Motion
picture actors and actresses–Biography–Juvenile literature. [1. Goldberg,
Whoopi, 1950– . 2. Comedians. 3. Actors and actresses. 4. Afro-
Americans–Biography–Juvenile literature. 5. Women–Biography.]
I. Title. II. Series: Ovations (Mankato, Minn.)

PN2287.G578D43   1999
791.43'028'092 [B]–dc21   97-50691

First edition

2   4   6   8   9   7   5   3   1

WHOOPI

GOLDBERG

BY JUDY DE BOER

Creative Education

REFLECTIONS

A spotlight shines on the center of a darkened stage. The audience eagerly waits for Whoopi Goldberg to begin her live performance. Suddenly, into the spotlight struts Whoopi, playing the part of Fontaine, a streetwise junkie thief with a Ph.D. in literature.

Fontaine distrusts people and swears a lot. He tells the audience about his trip to Amsterdam and his visit to the house where Anne Frank and her family hid from the Nazis during World War II. He finds himself crying in the empty room when he sees the words written by Anne Frank: "In spite of everything I still believe people are good at heart." He tells the audience, "I realized that life is a constant thing. It's constant live and learn. Never get over that."

Whoopi turns away from the audience and then turns back, this time as a seven-year-old girl. The girl is black and wears a white shirt on her head. "This is my long, luxurious blonde hair," says the girl. "Ain't it pretty? I want to have long blonde hair and blue eyes and be white so I can be on *The Love Boat*. But you've got to have blonde hair to be on *The Love Boat*." She wants to be white so bad that she sits in a bath of laundry bleach. By the end of her talk the audience is calling out to her, trying to convince her to take the shirt off her head, but she keeps it on.

Whoopi turns around once more and appears as a young woman who can't stand straight because the left side of her body is crippled. She tells us that she's going to get married in two weeks. "This man came to write about me. And at the end of my little tour he said, 'Gee, that was really interesting. What do you say we go have a drink and go dancing?' I said,

'Uh, no thank you.' And he said, 'Why not? Is it me?' I said, 'No, this is not a disco body.' And he said, 'Why not?' And I couldn't think of an answer, so I went dancing. I had a ball." She comes to the conclusion that normal is in the eye of the beholder, and she invites the audience to the wedding.

The stage goes dark. The house lights come up, and Whoopi Goldberg takes a bow. Her wide, bright smile flashes. She urges the audience to remember that dreams do come true because, as she has always said, "who in Chelsea thought they'd ever see the little Whoop up on Broadway?"

Whoopi Goldberg may be an entertainer of many faces, but she always wears the same wide smile whether at a Knicks game, opposite, on stage, or in public.

EVOLUTION

On November 13, 1955, in New York City, Emma Johnson gave birth to a daughter. As soon as she was born, as if holding a microphone, the baby put her thumb to her mouth. "My mom said she knew then that I was probably going to be an entertainer of some kind," Whoopi recalled years later. "I was ready to begin; they didn't even have to smack me. All they had to do was clean me up. I came out ready to function." Emma named her daughter Caryn.

Caryn grew up in the racially mixed Chelsea projects in lower Manhattan and decided on her future career early. "My first coherent thought was probably, I want to be an actor," she claimed later. Caryn spent hours in front of the television watching old movies and imagining herself on the

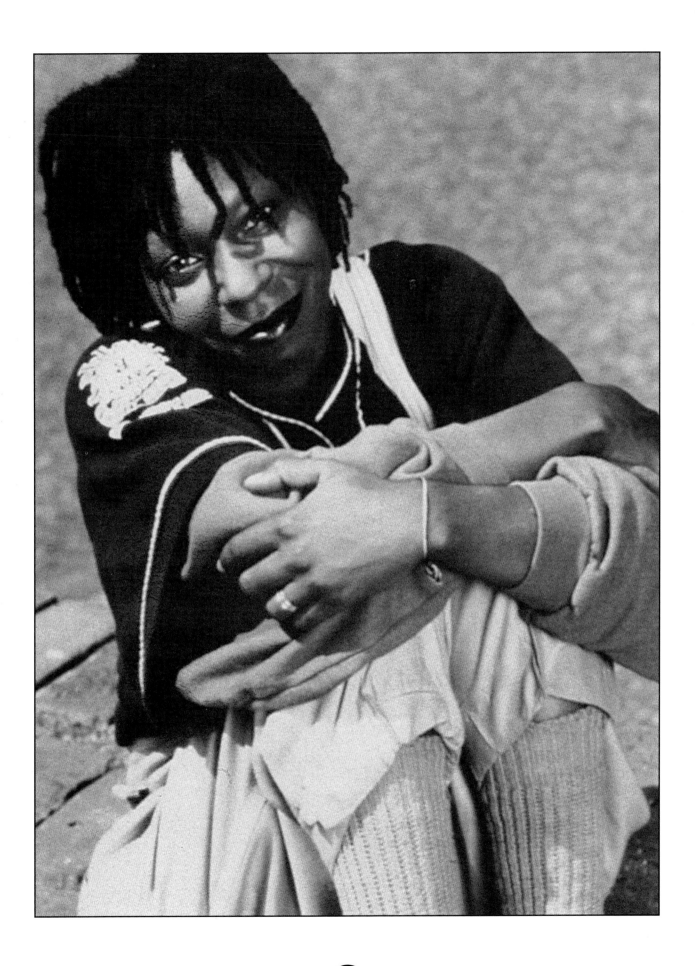

screen. Actors Carole Lombard, John Garfield, and Bette Davis were her friends, her mentors. By age eight, she was hooked.

Caryn began her formal acting training by joining a children's theater program at the Hudson Guild in New York. "I could be a princess, a teapot, a rabbit, anything," Whoopi said. From there, she satisfied her urge to perform by acting in local theater groups and auditioning for the Negro Ensemble Company. She also sang in the chorus of the Broadway musicals *Hair, Jesus Christ Superstar,* and *Pippin.*

But her childhood years had many hardships. Her father left the family when Caryn was very young, so Emma raised Caryn and her older brother, Clyde, alone on her nurse's salary and later as a Head Start teacher. Convinced by teachers and her own academic performance that she was abnormally slow, perhaps even mentally disabled, Caryn dropped out of high school. Years later, however, Caryn found out she had dyslexia, a learning disability that makes reading difficult. Dyslexia causes people to see words and letters in reverse order, such as "saw" for "was" or "b" for "d." Once Caryn realized that she wasn't stupid or slow, she learned how to deal with the disability and became an avid reader.

Whoopi credits much of her success to the love and support of her family: her mother Emma Johnson, left, and daughter Alexandrea, opposite.

After leaving high school in her teens, Caryn became involved in the hippie culture of the 1960s and began using drugs. She said she didn't use drugs because she was troubled, but simply "because the times were different." She has admitted to using heroin, LSD, uppers, downers, and marijuana, but she has little to say about that period in her life. She went through a long period of drug counseling, and today she takes every opportunity to speak out against drug use.

Caryn's rehabilitation resulted in more than just getting off drugs. She also married her rehab counselor and gave birth to a daughter, Alexandrea (named after Alexander the Great). The marriage didn't last, however. "I was in love, and that's why I got married," she explained. "It didn't work out. A lot of things don't work out." By the time she was twenty, she was single again, with a child to raise. It seemed time to move on.

With Alexandrea in tow, Caryn moved to San Diego, where she again focused on her acting career. She became a founding member of the San Diego Repertory Theater, joined an improvisational troupe called Spontaneous Combustion, and teamed up with another actor and worked in comedy clubs. She also changed her name. Whoopi explained that "it was a joke," saying, "First [my new name] was Whoopi Cushion. Then it was French, like Whoopi Cushon. My mother said, 'Nobody's gonna respect you with a name like that.' So I put Goldberg on it. Goldberg's a part of my family somewhere and that's all I can say about it." Whoopi Goldberg was born.

The time she spent trying to break into show business was difficult for Whoopi. To support herself and her daughter, she held numerous odd jobs, including bank teller and bricklayer. She even worked as a cosmetician in a mortuary. "It's not a bad job," she once said. "They can't talk back." Unfortunately, the jobs weren't enough and Whoopi applied for welfare. That experience was a difficult one. Years later, she said, "The greatest thing I ever was able to do was give a welfare check back."

From San Diego, Whoopi moved to Berkeley and joined the Blake Street Hawkeyes, a small theater company. She developed numerous characters and created her one-woman show, *The Spook Show*. Fontaine, the smart junkie thief, and the little black girl who dreams of having blonde hair and blue eyes are only two of her characters. They are, she said, "people who inhabit my body [and] are actually full-blooded people. I just kind of sit back and watch what they're up to. I become part of the audience."

A MAJOR BREAK

The *Spook Show* was an important turning point in Whoopi's career. She opened the show in San Francisco. It was such a success that she quickly took it on tour. She ended up playing an engagement at the *Dance Theater Workshop* in New York. There the show began to attract attention from critics. Whoopi also caught the eye of filmmaker Mike Nichols. He was so impressed with her work that he offered to produce her show on Broadway.

During the Broadway run of her show, in March 1984, Steven Spielberg called Whoopi. Spielberg had already become famous for directing the

Whoopi's acting career has included award-winning performances in live theater productions and motion pictures. Above, Whoopi is directed by legendary filmmaker Steven Spielberg.

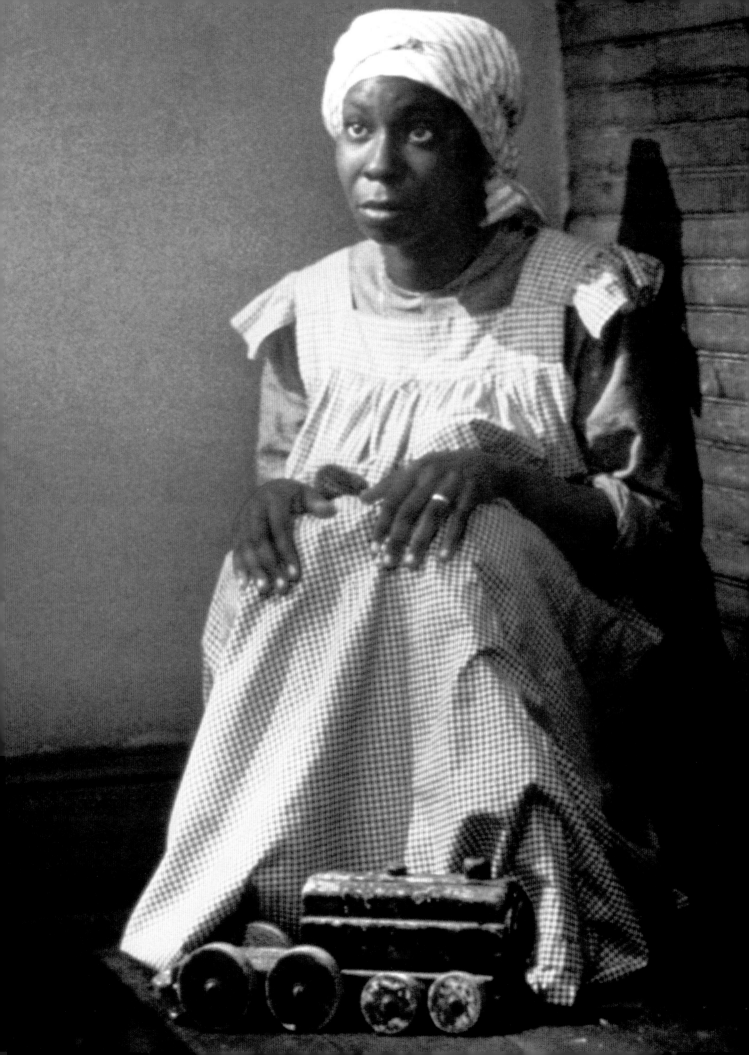

movies *Raiders of the Lost Ark* and
E.T.–The Extra-Terrestrial. He asked
Whoopi to perform her act for him and
several friends. She agreed, doing the
show just like she always did, with one
small addition. She added the character
Blee Tee, an extraterrestrial who lands
in Oakland and ends up on drugs and
in jail. Spielberg was impressed with
her humor and energy. He offered
Whoopi the lead in his upcoming film,
The Color Purple, a drama based on
the book by Alice Walker. Whoopi, who
had previously written to Walker asking
to be considered for a part if the novel
ever became a film, was ecstatic. "My
teeth caught cold cause all I could do
was grin," she said.

The Color Purple was filmed
during the summer of 1985. The story
centers on Celie, played by Goldberg,
who is physically and emotionally
abused by her father and then by her
husband. When a relationship between
Celie and a woman named Shug
develops, Celie discovers her inner
beauty and strength. For her work in
the film, Whoopi was nominated for
an Academy Award as Best Actress.

A series of films came
quickly on the heels
of Whoopi's movie success, but none
of these had the critical status of *The
Color Purple.* Whoopi took the films
that came her way but fought for roles
that she wanted to play. She wanted

*Whoopi realized
her childhood dream
of appearing on the
big screen when she
put forth an outstand-
ing performance in
the 1985 film* The
Color Purple.

to do it all—black roles, white roles, men, women. "I can make myself into anything," she said. "I am going to fight to do roles that people would never send to me, that they would never consider me for, because their state of thinking is not advanced. The country's thinking is advanced. The country can take anything."

SUPER STARDOM

Even with many box-office bombs, Whoopi kept working. In 1990, she made a triumphant return to the big screen with her Academy Award-winning performance as a kooky psychic in *Ghost*. In one of her next films, *Sister Act*, she played a singer hiding out in a convent to escape the mob. The film was such a success that a sequel was immediately written. Whoopi pushed hard to have the actresses from the original movie in the sequel, *Sister Act 2: Back in the Habit*, because she recognized their appeal to movie audiences.

Over the next few years, Whoopi continued to make movies targeted for younger audiences, but in 1996, Whoopie accepted the challenge of portraying Myrlie Evers, the widow of slain civil rights leader Medgar Evers in the film, *Ghosts of Mississippi*. This was an important role for Whoopi, one which firmly established her as a mature, serious dramatic actress.

Over the course of a decade, Whoopi Goldberg has showcased her acting talents in a variety of contexts, including drama, comedy, and science fiction.

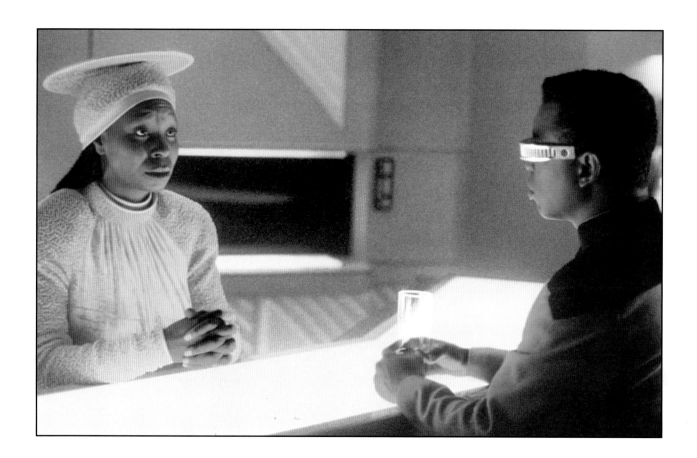

Whoopi has also done television work, including a recurring role in *"Star Trek: The Next Generation,"* where she played Guinan, an ancient survivor of a lost race of people who finds a home aboard the starship Enterprise. The Star Trek role came about at Whoopi's request. "I asked to be in it. They thought I was kidding. They couldn't understand why I wanted to do the show. I said, 'Listen, I'm a big fan of the show, that's why.' And they said, 'Great, we'll write you in.'" Guinan, one of the most popular Star Trek characters among fans of the series, even appeared in the seventh Star Trek movie, *Generations*.

In September 1992, Whoopi became the host of her own late-night talk show, though the show lasted only one season. She has won Emmy Award nominations for guest appearances on *"Moonlighting"* and *"A Different World,"* and her talents have been showcased on numerous TV specials, including *"Free To Be . . . A Family,"* *"FreedomFest: Nelson Mandela's 70th Birthday Special,"* and *"The Truth About Teachers."*

Throughout her career, the media has not always been happy with Whoopi and her work. Early on, critics compared Whoopi to successful comedians Lily Tomlin, Eddie Murphy, and Richard Pryor. Later, however, they criticized her for the roles she accepted. Yet even her strongest detractors have come full circle. In 1985 the National Association for the Advancement of Colored People (NAACP) criticized her work in *The Color Purple*. They said the movie portrayed black men in an unfavorable light. Yet in 1990 the organization named Whoopi Entertainer of the Year.

There are two things that set Whoopi Goldberg apart from many celebrities: her willingness to speak out for the rights of those in need and her childlike enthusiasm.

CONTINUING TO CARE

Many people in the film industry know Whoopi as a warm and caring person. She has a strong social conscience and is well known for her advocacy for women and children, the homeless, human rights, and the battle against AIDS. Her own experiences growing up in a single-parent family, as well as being a single parent herself, have had an impact on her views of parenthood and family. "Having a child so young may have given me the ability to look farther ahead," she revealed. "Everyone is selfish, but when you have a child, you can't be as selfish."

Whoopi became the center of much publicity when, in 1989, her 15-year-old daughter, Alexandrea, had a baby, a daughter named Amarah. While the tabloid newspapers tried to create a scandal, Whoopi's reaction

was calm. "Teenagers get pregnant all the time," she said. "Fortunately, she had a choice and she chose to be a parent. It wasn't forced on her. And I said, 'If that's what you want, I'll be there for you.'"

Whoopi firmly believes in family unity. "These things happen all over the world, all the time," she said, "and the only thing you can do is stand by your kids, whatever their decisions are." Whoopi now has a second granddaughter named Jerzey.

Whoopi's concern for children comes through in much of her work. She wrote *"Alice,"* a children's book, and has provided the voice of a character in the cartoon series *"Captain Planet and the Planeteers."* She also did a show, *"Tales from the Whoop,"* for the cable television station Nickelodeon. One of her most popular projects for children was providing the voice of Shenzi, the leader of the hyenas, in the Walt Disney film *The Lion King.* Her popularity with kids is reflected in the fact that she has won five Nickelodeon Kid's Choice Awards for Favorite Movie Actress.

Many organizations have recognized Whoopi's charitable work and have honored her with awards. One of her best-known contributions has been cohosting the annual *"Comic Relief"* benefits for the homeless. With cohosts Billy Crystal and Robin Williams, Whoopi has helped raise more than $30 million for homeless people around the country. She also participated in the televised *"Hurricane Relief"* benefit to aid victims of Hurricane Andrew in Florida.

Whoopi's personal life has had its ups and downs. She has been married four times. "My relationships haven't always been successful," she explained, "but when they haven't worked, it's been for lots of different reasons." One of those reasons is the pressure of being famous. Whoopi's relationships are scrutinized in the media and splashed across the covers of tabloids. Now that she's older, she would like to find someone who will share a caring, loving relationship with her.

Whoopi has made a tradition of teaming up with comedy icons Billy Crystal and Robin Williams for charity events.

In spite of the pressures of fame, Whoopi takes stardom casually and makes every attempt to live as normal a life as possible. When she wants to relax, she goes to her farm in Vermont and rides her horses.

When asked if she felt like a star, she replied, "I try not to. Sometimes it's fun, but sometimes it's a pain. And it's a lot of work—get dressed up, present yourself as a star is supposed to be presented. . . . And when you go out, you're going out as Whoopi Goldberg, and that's a bit wearing. But, you know, if you have to get milk, you have to get milk. I don't want to be trapped in my house."

Whoopi has come a long way from the projects of New York. By the late 1990s, she was one of the highest-paid women in Hollywood. Her journey, however, has been one of many struggles. With wit, courage, and style, she worked unceasingly toward her goals. "Even the down times were necessary for me," Whoopi said. "Even the bad times were productive. It's been a great ride . . . and it's getting better and better all the time."

Whoopi has handled all aspects of her fame—including autograph seekers and the receipt of prestigious awards—with unequalled enthusiasm.

V O I C E S

ON HER APPEARANCE:

"I'm cute! I'd go with me. It isn't always
what your face looks like."
Whoopi Goldberg

"She is very beautiful. Her smile is
wide and bright. Her pupils bleed with
the brown of her eyes, creating two
black holes—the kind scientists say are
sucking in our whole universe."
Actor Matthew Modine

"When they look at what is 'Western
beautiful,' I don't quite fit it. But sexy
is a state of mind."
Whoopi Goldberg

"She's had to deal with the you-don't-look-like-a-leading-lady syndrome in a system that's designed to recognize people who are her opposites. She has tenacity, will, and faith in herself."

     Bill Duke, director, Sister Act 2

O N   H E R   W O R K :

"Of all the reasons I wanted to do this film, working with Whoopi was the most attractive. Whoopi's a real giver as an actress, she's real unselfish, and she's still learning. She'll just keep getting better and better."

     Sam Elliott, costar, Fatal Beauty

"Whoopi has confidence in her own instincts. She's the closest thing to genius I've ever seen."

     Reuben Cannon, casting director

"I'm fighting the label of 'black' actress simply because it's very limiting in people's eyes, especially people who are making movies. I don't want them to say, 'Oh, she's a black actor, we can't use her.' I want them to say, 'Oh here's a great role. Call Meryl Streep. Call Diane Keaton. Call Whoopi Goldberg.'"

Whoopi Goldberg

"I can't think of an American actress who has Whoopi's comic ability and emotional depth. When I heard she wanted to do the part, I thought, Brilliant! Here's the edge. Now the piece has teeth."

Richard Benjamin, director,
Made in America

"Acting is my life's blood. I'd be in an institution if I weren't in the arts."

Whoopi Goldberg

Whoopi has appeared in productions that have bombed, soared, and won Oscars and critical acclaim. Top, she listens to Cleavon Little on her short-lived TV show **Baghdad Cafe.** *Some of her many movies include:* **Jumpin' Jack Flash,** *middle;* **Boys on the Side,** *opposite top; and* **Fatal Beauty,** *opposite bottom.*

ON HER PERSONALITY:

"Some of her affectations protect a sweetness inside. Her core—which is warm and kind—is surrounded by toughness and anger and her wanting to change the world. It's the mix that's so interesting and successful."

Jerry Zucker, director, Ghost

"I'm not going to try and change myself because other people are not comfortable with me. I'm comfortable with it. So why should I be uncomfortable to make other people feel better? That's not a good idea to me."

Whoopi Goldberg

Whoopi has appeared in a variety of roles, both on screen, (Soap Dish, *opposite*) and onstage (A Funny Thing Happened on the Way to the Forum, *below*).

"She has a gigantic spirit, and you're sort of slowly exposed to what she's like. Her compassion and her humanity are enormously moving and quite startling in somebody that funny. She has a way of cutting through everything, both personally and professionally. She just gets right to it."

Mike Nichols, director

"I just want people to think. I don't want people to take things at face value."

Whoopi Goldberg

Whoopi's Sister Act series and The Associate *were well-received at the box office. Opposite, Whoopi has made special appearances at Disneyland in Paris, and at Planet Hollywood in New York City.*

ON BEING FAMOUS:

"When I go out, I go as Whoopi Goldberg. But when I'm in the house, it's Caryn Johnson, Caryn Johnson parent, Caryn Johnson grandparent. . . . When I get home and turn into a real person who has to deal with bills and family crises and whatever, there's no room for Whoopi Goldberg in that."

Whoopi Goldberg

"She can't walk two steps down the street without being recognized and followed, with people screaming 'Hey Whoop! I love your movies!'"

An anonymous friend

ON HER PHILOSOPHY:

"I believe one person can make a difference, that we are responsible for other people. You know, peace and love. It's out of fashion, but it's really a great way to live."

Whoopi Goldberg

"I will speak out for the things I believe in. People seem to listen a little bit. And I do want things to get better."

Whoopi Goldberg

"I just know I'm one of the luckiest people on earth."

Whoopi Goldberg

"I was so happy [to turn 40]. I finally felt like I was growing into myself. I'm now growing into my face and growing into my thoughts, and I'm clearer about a lot of things."

Whoopi Goldberg

Whoopi uses her celebrity status to draw attention to issues important to her. Below, Whoopi has also shared her life story in print, publishing a humorous autobiography in 1997.

OVATIONS